ASTHMA EDUCATION FOR HEALTH CARE PROVIDERS

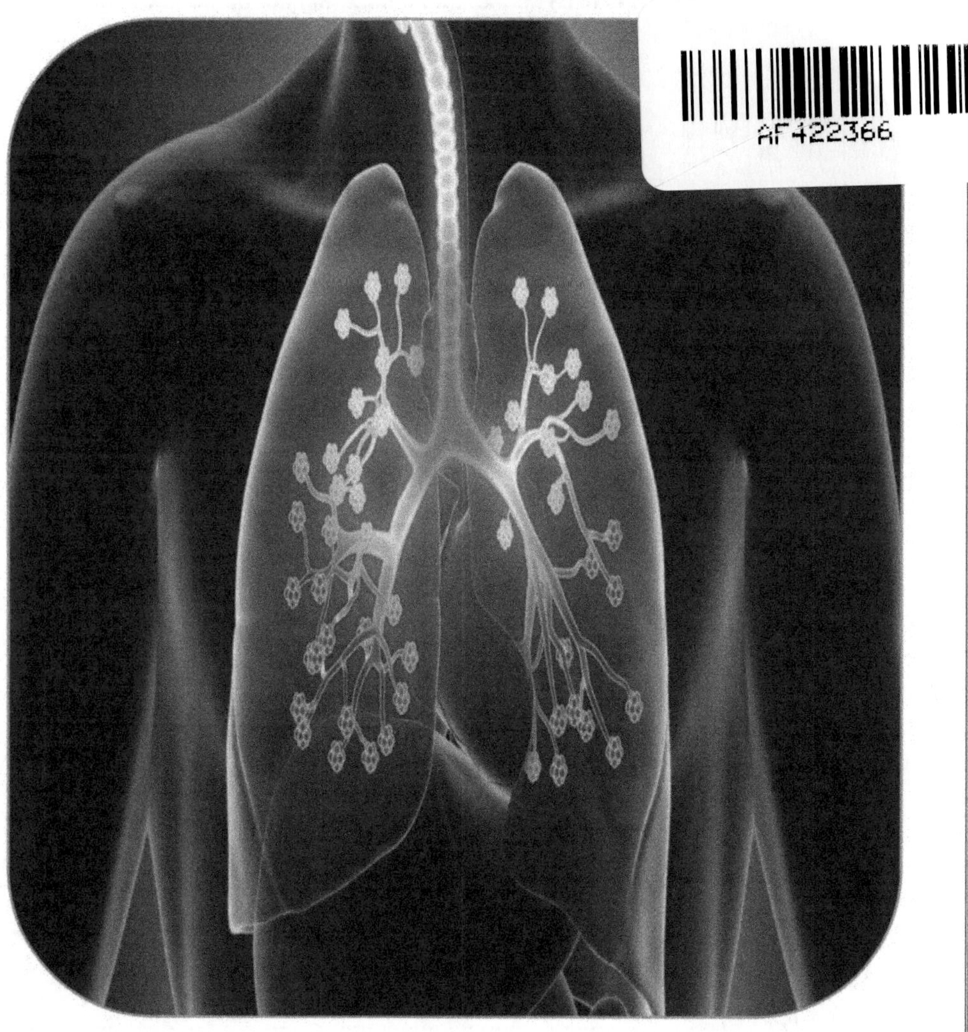

TABLE OF CONTENTS

COURSE OVERVIEW

This course explores the essential elements of delivering high-quality, guideline-based asthma care and measuring its impact on patient outcomes. Participants will gain a profound comprehension of the latest clinical practice guidelines for asthma management and strategies for implementing these evidence-based recommendations into clinical practice. The course will also cover best practices for systematically measuring and improving asthma-related outcomes to drive continuous quality improvement.

COURSE OBJECTIVE

Healthcare providers will gain comprehensive knowledge and practical skills in asthma management, from diagnosis to treatment and patient education, enabling them to improve patient outcomes.

COURSE MATERIALS

To learn this course, **healthcare providers/ participants** must be provided with materials like a Pen, pencil, notebook, and notepad to better understand and make it easy for them to learn.

INTRODUCTION

Asthma is a prevalent long-term respiratory ailment that impacts millions of individuals globally. Effective management of asthma is crucial for improving patient outcomes, reducing hospital admissions, and enhancing the quality of life for those living with this condition. One key aspect of successful asthma care is the implementation of evidence-based clinical practice guidelines. This course is designed to provide healthcare providers with comprehensive knowledge and practical skills in asthma management, utilizing a project-based learning approach.

By the end of this course, healthcare providers will be well-equipped to diagnose, treat, and manage asthma in patients of all ages. The course is structured into six modules, each focusing on a critical aspect of asthma care. Through a combination of theoretical knowledge, real-world examples, hands-on activities, and scenarios, participants will gain a thorough understanding of asthma and its management.

MODULE ONE

LESSON ONE: Understanding the Pathophysiology of Asthma

Asthma is an ongoing inflammatory condition of the airways. Particularly at night or in the early morning, the inflammation causes recurring episodes of coughing, dyspnea, chest tightness, and wheezing. These episodes are typically linked to a diffuse but fluctuating blockage of airflow in the lung, which is frequently reversible with treatment or on its own. The underlying pathophysiology of asthma involves complex interactions between inflammatory cells, mediators, and structural cells in the airways. This chronic inflammation leads to airway hyperresponsiveness, where the airways are hypersensitive and constrict excessively in response to a variety of stimuli. Common asthma triggers include allergens, respiratory infections, exercise, cold air, stress, and certain medications.

Key Components of Asthma Pathophysiology

1. **Airway Inflammation**
   - Chronic inflammation of the airways involving different inflammatory cells, such as eosinophils, mast cells, T-lymphocytes, and neutrophils, is a characteristic of asthma.
   - These inflammatory cells release numerous mediators, including histamine, leukotrienes, prostaglandins, and cytokines, which drive the inflammatory process.
   - The chronic inflammation leads to damage and remodeling of the airway epithelium.
2. **Airway Hyperresponsiveness**
   - A key feature of asthma is increased sensitivity and hyperresponsiveness of the airways to various stimuli.

- This airway hyperresponsiveness causes the smooth muscle in the airways to constrict excessively in response to triggers, leading to bronchoconstriction.
- Triggers can include allergens, irritants, exercise, cold air, respiratory infections, and certain medications.

3. **Reversible Airflow Obstruction**
   - The combination of airway inflammation and hyperresponsiveness results in a variable and often reversible airflow obstruction.
   - During an asthma exacerbation, the airways become further inflamed and constricted, resulting in the characteristic wheezing, chest tightness, and shortness of breath.
   - The airflow obstruction is often (but not always) reversible with appropriate treatment or spontaneously.

4. **Airway Remodeling**
   - Over time, chronic inflammation can lead to structural changes in the airways, known as airway remodeling.
   - This includes thickening of the airway smooth muscle, increased deposition of extracellular matrix proteins, and goblet cell hyperplasia.
   - Airway remodeling can contribute to persistent airflow limitation and reduced responsiveness to treatments.
   - Understanding this underlying pathophysiology is crucial for the effective management and treatment of asthma in clinical practice.

LESSON TWO: IDENTIFYING COMMON TRIGGERS AND SYMPTOMS OF ASTHMA

Asthma symptoms might differ in severity and frequency. Recognizing these symptoms early can prevent exacerbations and improve management.

Common Symptoms:

- Wheezing: A high-pitched whistling noise made during breathing, particularly when exhaling.
- Shortness of Breath: Difficulty in breathing or feeling breathless.
- Chest Tightness: A constriction or pressure in the chest
- Coughing: Often worse at night or early in the morning and might be the only symptom.

Common Triggers:

- Allergens - Dust mites, pet dander, pollen, mold, and other allergens can trigger asthma symptoms.
- Exercise -Certain individuals with asthma may be triggered by physical activity and exercise.
- Weather changes - Cold air, dry air, and changes in weather patterns can provoke asthma symptoms.
- Irritants - Smoke, strong smells, air pollution, and certain chemicals can irritate the airways.
- Emotions - Stress, anxiety, and strong emotional responses can induce asthma symptoms.
- Medications - Certain medications like aspirin, beta-blockers, and NSAIDs can trigger asthma in some patients.

LESSON THREE: DIFFERENTIATING ASTHMA FROM OTHER RESPIRATORY CONDITIONS

While asthma shares symptoms with several other respiratory conditions, there are distinct features and diagnostic methods to differentiate it.

Common Respiratory Conditions to Differentiate from Asthma

1. **Chronic Obstructive Pulmonary Disease (COPD)**
   - **Symptoms**: Persistent cough, sputum production, and dyspnea, mainly affecting older adults and smokers.

- **Differences:** COPD is characterized by irreversible airflow limitation, whereas asthma is usually reversible. COPD also tends to worsen over time.
- **Diagnostic Tools:** Spirometry, showing a reduced FEV1/FVC ratio without significant reversibility after bronchodilator use.

2. **Bronchitis**
   - **Symptoms:** Persistent cough, mucus production, and fatigue.
   - **Differences:** Bronchitis, especially acute bronchitis, often follows a viral infection and resolves over time. Chronic bronchitis is a component of COPD.
   - **Diagnostic Tools:** History and physical examination, sputum culture if infection is suspected.

3. **Vocal Cord Dysfunction (VCD)**
   - **Symptoms:** Similar to asthma, including wheezing and shortness of breath, but often triggered by speaking, laughing, or exercise.
   - **Differences:** VCD involves the vocal cords closing improperly, which is often mistaken for asthma. Symptoms do not respond to typical asthma medications.
   - **Diagnostic Tools:** Laryngoscopy to visualize vocal cord movement.

4. **Heart Failure**
   - **Symptoms:** Shortness of breath, wheezing, and coughing, particularly at night or when lying down.
   - **Differences:** Often associated with additional symptoms like edema, weight gain, and fatigue. Asthma symptoms typically worsen with exposure to triggers and are not usually related to fluid overload.
   - **Diagnostic Tools:** Echocardiogram, BNP levels, and history of cardiac disease.

5. **Gastroesophageal Reflux Disease (GERD)**
   - **Symptoms:** Heartburn, regurgitation, and chronic cough, which can mimic asthma symptoms.

- **Differences:** GERD-related asthma symptoms are often worse at night and may be relieved by antacids.
- **Diagnostic Tools:** pH monitoring, esophagogastroduodenoscopy (EGD).

Scenario: A 35-year-old woman comes in with chest tightness, dyspnea, and sporadic wheezing, especially at night. She reports increased symptoms during the spring and after visiting a friend's house with a cat. She has a history of atopic dermatitis and allergic rhinitis.

Activity: Symptom Identification Exercise

Step-by-Step Directions

- Read the Case Study: Understand the patient's history and presenting symptoms.
- List the Symptoms: Identify which symptoms are indicative of asthma.
- Compare Symptoms: Distinguish these symptoms from those of other conditions such as COPD or GERD.
- Identify Triggers: Determine the potential asthma triggers from the patient's history.

DISCUSSION QUESTIONS:

- What are the most common triggers of asthma in your clinical experience?
- How can you differentiate between asthma and other respiratory conditions?

MODULE TWO

LESSON ONE: IMPLEMENTING LIFESTYLE MODIFICATIONS AND ENVIRONMENTAL CONTROLS TO MANAGE ASTHMA

Non-pharmacological interventions play a critical role in managing asthma by reducing exposure to triggers and promoting overall health.

LIFESTYLE MODIFICATIONS

1. **Exercise:** Regular physical activity can improve overall lung function and cardiovascular health. However, patients should choose activities that do not trigger their asthma and may benefit from a pre-exercise bronchodilator if exercise-induced bronchoconstriction is an issue.
   - **Recommendations:** Encourage activities like swimming, walking, and cycling. Advise a gradual warm-up before vigorous exercise and a cool-down period afterward.
2. **Diet:** Lean meats, healthy grains, fruits, and vegetables all contribute to a balanced diet that boosts immunity and lowers inflammation.
   - **Recommendations:** Promote a diet rich in omega-3 fatty acids and antioxidants, which are present in foods like nuts, seeds, and seafood. Advise patients to maintain a healthy weight, as obesity can worsen asthma symptoms.
3. **Stress Management:** Anxiety and stress can make asthma symptoms worse. Stress management methods include deep breathing, meditation, and yoga.
   - **Recommendations:** Suggest incorporating stress-reducing activities into daily routines and considering professional counseling if necessary.

ENVIRONMENTAL CONTROLS

1. **Allergen Avoidance:** Reducing exposure to allergens such as dust mites, pollen, mold, pet dander, and cockroach droppings can significantly improve asthma control.
   - Recommendations: Use dust-proof mattress and pillow covers, wash bedding weekly in hot water, maintain low indoor humidity, use air purifiers, and keep pets out of bedrooms.
2. **Irritant Control:** Avoiding irritants such as tobacco smoke, strong odors, and air pollution is essential.
   - **Recommendations:** Advise patients not to smoke and to avoid secondhand smoke, use unscented cleaning products, and monitor air quality reports to limit outdoor activities on high pollution days.
3. **Home Environment:** Maintaining a clean and well-ventilated home can reduce asthma triggers.
   - **Recommendations:** Regularly clean carpets, drapes, and upholstery; repair water leaks promptly to prevent mold; and ensure proper ventilation in kitchens and bathrooms.

LESSON TWO: RECOGNIZING THE ROLE OF COMORBID CONDITIONS IN ASTHMA MANAGEMENT

Comorbid conditions can complicate asthma management and must be addressed to optimize treatment outcomes.

Common Comorbid Conditions

1. **ALLERGIC RHINITIS**
   - **Impact:** Nasal inflammation can worsen asthma symptoms and complicate management.
   - **Management:** Use intranasal corticosteroids, antihistamines, and allergen avoidance strategies.

2. **GASTROESOPHAGEAL REFLUX DISEASE (GERD)**
   - **Impact:** Acid reflux can trigger bronchoconstriction and exacerbate asthma.
   - **Management:** Lifestyle modifications (e.g., elevating the head of the bed, avoiding late meals), antacids, and proton pump inhibitors.
3. **OBESITY**
   - **Impact:** Excess weight can worsen asthma symptoms and reduce lung function.
   - **Management:** Encourage weight loss through diet, exercise, and behavioral interventions.
4. **SLEEP APNEA**
   - **Impact:** Disrupted sleep can lead to poor asthma control and daytime fatigue.
   - **Management:** Use continuous positive airway pressure (CPAP) therapy, weight loss, and sleep hygiene practices.
5. **ANXIETY AND DEPRESSION**
   - **Impact:** Mental health conditions can affect asthma control and medication adherence.
   - **Management:** Provide psychological support, consider counseling, and address both conditions concurrently.

LESSON THREE: DEVELOPING STRATEGIES TO IMPROVE PATIENT ADHERENCE TO TREATMENT PLANS

Adherence to treatment plans is crucial for effective asthma management. Here are strategies to enhance adherence:

EDUCATIONAL STRATEGIES

1. **Clear Communication:** Use simple, non-technical language to explain the importance of adherence and how each part of the treatment plan works.
   - **Recommendations:** Use visual aids, demonstrations, and teach-back methods to ensure understanding.

2. **Personalized Education:** Tailor education to each patient's needs, preferences, and literacy levels.
   - **Recommendations:** Provide written materials, videos, and interactive tools that match the patient's learning style.

BEHAVIORAL STRATEGIES

1. **Goal Setting:** Collaboratively set achievable goals for asthma management and track progress.
   - **Recommendations:** Use SMART goals (Specific, Measurable, Achievable, Relevant, Time-bound) and celebrate milestones.
2. **Reminders and Follow-Up:** Use reminders such as phone alerts, apps, or follow-up calls to encourage adherence.
   - **Recommendations:** Schedule regular follow-up appointments to review progress and adjust the treatment plan as needed.

SUPPORT STRATEGIES

1. **Family and Peer Support:** Involve family members and peers in the patient's care to provide encouragement and assistance.
   - **Recommendations:** Educate family members about asthma and the importance of supporting the patient's adherence to their treatment plan.
2. **Self-Management Programs:** Enroll patients in asthma self-management programs that provide ongoing education and support.
   - **Recommendations:** Use programs that offer coaching, group sessions, and resources for continuous learning.

Scenario: A 50-year-old male with severe persistent asthma struggles with adherence to his treatment plan, leading to frequent exacerbations. He has comorbid GERD and obesity.

Activity: Adherence Improvement Strategy Development

Step-by-Step Directions

- Assess Barriers: Identify the patient's specific barriers to adherence, such as medication side effects, misunderstanding of the treatment plan, or lifestyle factors.
- Educational Intervention: Provide personalized education on the importance of adherence and how to manage side effects. Use visual aids and interactive tools.
- Behavioral Intervention: Set achievable goals with the patient, such as tracking symptoms daily and using medication reminders.
- Support Intervention: Involve the patient's family in the education process and provide information on local support groups or self-management programs.

DISCUSSION QUESTIONS

- What are the most common barriers to asthma medication adherence?
- How can you tailor their approach to improve adherence in different patient populations?

MODULE THREE

LESSON ONE: RECOGNIZING SIGNS OF AN ASTHMA EXACERBATION AND PROVIDING APPROPRIATE EMERGENCY CARE

Asthma exacerbations can be life-threatening if not managed promptly and effectively. Healthcare providers must be able to identify the signs of an exacerbation and initiate appropriate emergency care.

SIGNS OF AN ASTHMA EXACERBATION

1. **Mild To Moderate Exacerbations**
   - **Symptoms:** Increased shortness of breath, wheezing, chest tightness, and cough.
   - **Physical Findings:** Tachypnea (rapid breathing), use of accessory muscles for breathing, mild tachycardia (increased heart rate).

2. **Severe Exacerbations**
   - **Symptoms:** Severe shortness of breath, difficulty speaking in full sentences, significant chest tightness, and cyanosis (bluish tint to the skin).
   - **Physical Findings:** Severe tachypnea, significant use of accessory muscles, decreased breath sounds, and signs of fatigue or confusion.

3. **Life-Threatening Exacerbations**
   - **Symptoms:** Extreme difficulty breathing, inability to speak more than a few words, altered mental status, and unresponsiveness.
   - **Physical Findings:** Cyanosis, absence of breath sounds, bradycardia (slow heart rate), and hypotension (low blood pressure).

EMERGENCY CARE FOR ASTHMA EXACERBATIONS

1. **Initial Assessment**
   - Rapid Evaluation: Assess airway, breathing, and circulation (ABCs). Measure peak expiratory flow (PEF) if possible.
   - History and Examination: Quickly gather history of the current exacerbation, previous exacerbations, and response to medications. Perform a focused physical examination.
2. **Oxygen Therapy**
   - Supplemental Oxygen: Administer oxygen to maintain SpO2 (oxygen saturation) $\geq 94\%$.
3. **Medication Administration**
   - Short-Acting Beta-Agonists (SABAs): Administer inhaled bronchodilators (e.g., albuterol) via nebulizer or metered-dose inhaler (MDI) with a spacer. Repeat doses every 20 minutes for up to 1 hour.
   - Corticosteroids: Administer systemic corticosteroids (e.g., prednisone) to reduce airway inflammation.
   - Anticholinergics: Consider adding inhaled anticholinergics (e.g., ipratropium) for additional bronchodilation.
4. **Monitoring and Reassessment**
   - Continuous Monitoring: Monitor vital signs, oxygen saturation, and patient response to treatment. Reassess every 15-30 minutes.
   - Hospital Admission: Consider hospital admission for patients with severe or life-threatening exacerbations, those not responding to initial treatment, or those with high-risk factors (e.g., previous intubation, frequent exacerbations).

LESSON TWO: DEVELOPING FOLLOW-UP CARE PLANS TO PREVENT FUTURE EXACERBATIONS

Effective follow-up care is essential to prevent future exacerbations and ensure long-term asthma control. Follow-up care plans should be comprehensive and individualized.

COMPONENTS OF FOLLOW-UP CARE PLANS

1. **Scheduled Follow-Up Visits**
   - Frequency: Schedule follow-up visits based on the severity of asthma and recent exacerbations. Typically, follow-ups are every 1-6 months.
   - Purpose: Review asthma control, assess adherence to the treatment plan, and adjust medications as needed.

2. **Patient Education**
   - Reinforcement: Reinforce education on asthma management, including trigger avoidance, proper inhaler technique, and adherence to medications.
   - Updates: Provide updates on new asthma management guidelines and any changes in the patient's treatment plan.

3. **Action Plan Review**
   - Review and Revise: Review the patient's asthma action plan at each visit. Revise the plan based on changes in symptoms, triggers, and treatment response.
   - Teach-Back Method: Use the teach-back method to ensure the patient understands how to use the action plan effectively.

4. **Monitoring Tools**
   - Peak Flow Monitoring: To assess lung function, encourage regular use of a peak flow meter and detect early signs of worsening asthma.
   - Symptom Diary: Have patients keep a symptom diary to track asthma symptoms, triggers, and medication use.

5. **Referral and Support**
   - Specialist Referral: Refer patients to an asthma specialist if their asthma is not well controlled or if they have complex comorbid conditions.
   - Support Groups: Provide information on local or online support groups for patients with asthma.

ACTIVITIES FOR FOLLOW-UP CARE

- Role-Playing: Practice follow-up visit scenarios to improve skills in patient education, action plan review, and treatment adjustment.
- Peer Review: Review follow-up care plans with peers to identify strengths and areas for improvement.

LESSON THREE: EVALUATING AND ADJUSTING ASTHMA MANAGEMENT PLANS BASED ON PATIENT PROGRESS

Ongoing evaluation and adjustment of asthma management plans are crucial for achieving and maintaining optimal asthma control.

STEPS FOR EVALUATION AND ADJUSTMENT

1. **Assessment of Asthma Control**
   - Symptom Review: Ask about the frequency and severity of daytime and nighttime symptoms, use of rescue medications, and activity limitations.
   - Objective Measures: Use spirometry or peak flow measurements to assess lung function.
2. **Identification of Barriers**
   - Adherence Issues: Identify any issues with medication adherence or incorrect inhaler technique.
   - Trigger Exposure: Assess for continued exposure to known asthma triggers.

3. **Adjustment of Treatment Plan**
   - Step-Up Therapy: Increase medication doses or add additional therapies for patients with poor asthma control.
   - Step-Down Therapy: For patients with well-controlled asthma, reduce medication doses or simplify the treatment plan for at least three months.
4. **Patient Education and Support**
   - Reinforce Education: Provide ongoing education on asthma management, medication use, and trigger avoidance.
   - Motivational Interviewing: Use motivational interviewing techniques to address barriers to adherence and enhance patient engagement.
5. **Regular Follow-Up**
   - Scheduled Visits: Schedule regular follow-up visits to monitor progress and make further adjustments as needed.
   - Telemedicine: Utilize telemedicine for more frequent check-ins and to address concerns promptly.

ACTIVITIES FOR EVALUATION AND ADJUSTMENT

- Case Reviews: Analyze patient cases to identify effective strategies for adjusting treatment plans based on patient progress.
- Mock Evaluations: Conduct mock evaluations of asthma management plans and practice making adjustments based on simulated patient data.

SCENARIO: A 45-year-old female with severe asthma has had multiple exacerbations in the past year. Her follow-up care plan needs to be revised to prevent future exacerbations.

Activity: Follow-Up Care Plan Development and Adjustment

Step-by-Step Directions

- **Initial Assessment:** Conduct a thorough assessment of her asthma control, including reviewing symptoms, triggers, and lung function tests.

- **Identify Barriers:** Discuss any barriers to adherence, such as medication side effects or difficulties using inhalers.
- **Adjust Treatment Plan:** Increase the dosage of her inhaled corticosteroids and add a long-acting beta-agonist. Provide additional education on trigger avoidance.
- **Develop a Follow-Up Plan**: Schedule follow-up visits every two months to monitor progress. Encourage the use of a peak flow meter and a symptom diary.
- **Evaluate and Reassess:** At each follow-up visit, reassess her asthma control and make further adjustments as needed. Use motivational interviewing to enhance adherence.

DISCUSSION QUESTIONS

- What are the key elements of an effective follow-up care plan for asthma patients?
- As a healthcare provider, how can you effectively evaluate and adjust asthma management plans?

MODULE FOUR

LESSON ONE: CLASSIFYING ASTHMA SEVERITY

Asthma severity is typically classified into the following categories based on the patient's symptoms and lung function:

1. **Intermittent Asthma**
   - Symptoms occur ≤ 2 days per week
   - Nighttime symptoms occur ≤ 2 times per month
   - Lung function (FEV1 or PEF) is >80% of predicted
2. **Mild Persistent Asthma**
   - Symptoms occur > 2 days per week but not daily
   - Nighttime symptoms occur > 2 times per month
   - Lung function (FEV1 or PEF) is >80% of predicted
3. **Moderate Persistent Asthma**
   - Daily symptoms
   - Nighttime symptoms occur > 1 time per week
   - Lung function (FEV1 or PEF) is 60-80% of predicted
4. **Severe Persistent Asthma**
   - Continuous symptoms
   - Frequent nighttime symptoms
   - Lung function (FEV1 or PEF) is <60% of predicted

The classification helps guide the appropriate treatment approach:

- Intermittent and mild persistent asthma are typically treated with as-needed quick-relief medications.
- Moderate and severe persistent asthma require daily controller medications like inhaled corticosteroids.
- Severe persistent asthma may also require add-on therapies like biologics.

Periodic assessment of symptoms and lung function is important to monitor asthma control and adjust treatment accordingly.

ASSESSING ASTHMA CONTROL

Achieving and maintaining well-controlled asthma is the goal of treatment. Frequent assessment and adjustments to the treatment plan are often needed to reach this target. Assessing asthma control is an important part of managing the condition. Here are the key factors to consider when evaluating asthma control:

1. **Daytime Symptoms**
   - How often do you experience symptoms like wheezing, coughing, chest tightness, or shortness of breath?
   - Ideally, these should occur ≤ 2 days per week for well-controlled asthma.

2. **Nighttime Symptoms**
   - How often do asthma symptoms disrupt your sleep?
   - Nighttime symptoms should occur <2 nights per month for well-controlled asthma.

3. **Use of Rescue Medications**
   - How often do you need to use your quick-relief ("rescue") inhaler?
   - For well-controlled asthma, rescue inhaler use should be ≤ 2 days per week.

4. **Lung Function**
   - Spirometry or peak flow measurements can assess lung function objectively.
   - For well-controlled asthma, FEV1 or PEF should be $>80\%$ of the predicted value.

5. **Exacerbations**
   - How many asthma attacks or flare-ups have you had that required oral steroids or hospitalization?
   - Well-controlled asthma has ≤ 1 exacerbation per year.

Based on these factors, asthma can be classified as:

- Well-controlled
- Partly controlled
- Uncontrolled

LESSON TWO: QUICK-RELIEF MEDICATIONS (BRONCHODILATORS)

Bronchodilators are asthma drugs that act by relaxing and opening the airways, providing quick relief or rescue. The two main types of bronchodilators used for asthma are:

1. **Short-Acting Beta-Agonists (SABAs)**
    - Examples: albuterol (Ventolin, Proair), levalbuterol (Xopenex)
    - Provide rapid (within minutes) but short-acting (4-6 hours) relief of asthma symptoms
    - Used as needed for symptom relief or prior to exercise
2. **Long-Acting Beta-Agonists (LABAs)**
    - Examples: salmeterol (Serevent), formoterol (Foradil)
    - Provide longer-lasting (12 hours) bronchodilation
    - It should not be used as sole therapy but rather in combination with an inhaled corticosteroid
    - Used for daily maintenance treatment of persistent asthma

The key differences between SABAs and LABAs are

- The onset of action: SABAs work within minutes, and LABAs take 15-20 minutes
- Duration of action: SABAs last 4-6 hours, LABAs last 12 hours
- Purpose: SABAs for quick relief, LABAs for daily maintenance

Overuse of SABA rescue inhalers may be a sign of poorly controlled asthma and the need to step up daily controller therapy. Patients should be counseled on proper inhaler technique and the role of both quick-relief and long-term controller medications.

PROPER INHALER TECHNIQUE

Proper inhaler technique is crucial for ensuring optimal medication delivery and asthma control. Here are the key steps for using common asthma inhalers correctly:

1. **Metered-Dose Inhalers (MDIs):**
   - Remove the cap and shake the inhaler well.
   - Hold the inhaler upright with your thumb on the bottom and your index finger on top.
   - Breathe out fully.
   - Close your lips around the mouthpiece after placing it in your mouth.
   - Begin breathing in slowly and deeply through your mouth.
   - As you start breathing in, press down on the top of the inhaler to release one puff.
   - Continue breathing in slowly and deeply for 5-10 seconds.
   - After holding your breath for ten seconds, gently release it.
   - Wait 1 minute before taking a second puff, if needed.
2. Dry Powder Inhalers (DPIs)
   - Open the inhaler and load the dose.
   - Exhale fully away from the mouthpiece.
   - Place the mouthpiece between your lips and inhale rapidly and deeply.
   - Breathe in for five to ten seconds, then gently release it.

Additional Tips

- Use a spacer or holding chamber with an MDI to improve medication delivery.
- To avoid oral thrush, rinse your mouth with water after using an inhaler that contains corticosteroids.
- Replace inhaler caps when not in use to keep the mouthpiece clean.
- Replace inhalers when the counter reaches zero or as directed.

DISCUSSION QUESTIONS

- What strategies can healthcare providers implement to ensure patients use their inhalers correctly?
- What strategies can you implement to ensure patients use their inhalers correctly?

MODULE FIVE

LESSON ONE: ASTHMA IN CHILDREN

Asthma management in children requires a tailored approach to address the unique considerations and challenges. Here are some key aspects of asthma care in the pediatric population:

1. **Developmental Factors**
   - Adjust medication dosing and delivery devices based on the child's age and size.
   - Consider the child's ability to use inhalers and spacers properly.
   - Provide age-appropriate education and engage the family in the treatment plan.
2. **Diagnostic Approach**
   - Obtain a detailed history of symptoms and family history.
   - Use lung function testing, such as spirometry, when feasible.
   - Consider additional testing, like allergy evaluation, if indicated.
3. **Trigger Management**
   - Identify and minimize exposure to common pediatric asthma triggers, such as viral infections, allergens, and air pollution.
   - Educate families on environmental control measures, such as using air filters and reducing exposure to tobacco smoke.
4. **Medication Management**
   - Prefer inhaled corticosteroids as the foundation of daily control therapy.
   - Consider the use of leukotriene receptor antagonists as an alternative or add-on therapy.
   - Ensure proper inhaler technique and use of spacer devices.
5. **Adherence and Self-Management**
   - Engage children and their families in the development of the asthma action plan.

- Provide age-appropriate education on the importance of adherence and symptom monitoring.
- Encourage shared decision-making and empower children to participate in their care.

6. **Comorbidities and Complications**
   - Monitor for and manage conditions that can complicate asthma, such as allergic rhinitis, obesity, and gastroesophageal reflux disease.
   - Consider the potential impact of asthma on the child's physical, emotional, and social well-being.

7. **Transition to Adult Care**
   - Develop a plan for the smooth transition of care from pediatric to adult asthma management.
   - Educate adolescents on the importance of self-management and the need for ongoing care.

Effective asthma management in children requires a collaborative approach between healthcare providers, families, and the child. Ongoing monitoring, education, and tailored treatment strategies are essential for achieving optimal asthma control and improving long-term outcomes.

LESSON TWO: ASTHMA IN THE ELDERLY

Asthma management in the elderly population requires careful consideration of the unique challenges and clinical characteristics associated with this age group. Here are some key aspects to address when caring for older adults with asthma:

1. **Diagnostic Considerations**
   - Asthma can be underdiagnosed or misdiagnosed in the elderly due to overlap with other respiratory conditions, such as COPD.
   - Obtain a thorough medical history and perform objective lung function testing, including reversibility assessments.

- Consider alternative or additional diagnostic tests, such as chest imaging or bronchial provocation, if needed.

2. **Comorbidities and Polypharmacy**
   - Heart disease, diabetes, and cognitive impairment are just a few of the many comorbid medical issues that older persons with asthma frequently have.
   - Carefully evaluate potential drug interactions and side effects, especially with inhaled corticosteroids.
   - To guarantee safe and efficient medication administration, coordinate care with other healthcare professionals.

3. **Inhaler Technique and Adherence**
   - Assess the patient's physical and cognitive abilities to properly use inhalation devices.
   - Provide hands-on training and regular re-evaluation of inhaler technique.
   - Address any barriers to adherence, such as dexterity, vision, or memory issues.

4. **Exacerbation Risk and Management**
   - The risk of asthma in older persons is increased for severe exacerbations and asthma-related hospitalizations.
   - Ensure appropriate use of rescue medications and have a clear plan for accessing emergency care.
   - Consider the use of biologics or oral corticosteroids for severe, uncontrolled asthma.

5. **Lifestyle and Environmental Factors**
   - Evaluate the impact of factors such as physical activity, nutrition, and social isolation on asthma control.
   - Guide home environmental modifications to reduce exposures and trigger avoidance.

6. **Psychosocial Considerations**
   - Take care of any mental health issues, such as anxiety or depression, that can impact asthma management.
   - Engage family members or caregivers to support the patient's self-management and adherence.

7. **Tailored Treatment Approaches**
   - Consider lower starting doses of inhaled corticosteroids and slower titration to minimize side effects.
   - Prefer once-daily dosing regimens to simplify the medication routine.
   - Monitor for and address any adverse effects, such as osteoporosis or cataracts.

Elderly asthma patients need comprehensive, patient-centered care that takes a multidisciplinary approach to address their particular needs and challenges of this population. Ongoing monitoring, education, and collaborative decision-making are essential for optimizing asthma control and quality of life.

DISCUSSION QUESTIONS

- How can healthcare providers effectively educate both children with asthma and their families to ensure proper medication use and adherence to the asthma action plan?
- Discuss the role of family engagement in managing pediatric asthma and strategies to empower children to participate actively in their asthma treatment as they grow older.

MODULE SIX

LESSON ONE: IMPLEMENTING GUIDELINE-BASED CARE

Implementing guideline-based care is crucial for providing high-quality, evidence-based asthma management. Strategies for effectively implementing guideline-based asthma care are:

1. **Disseminate and Educate**
   - As a healthcare provider, you should be aware of the latest asthma management guidelines.
   - Encourage participation in continuing medical education (CME) activities focused on asthma management.

2. **Standardize Clinical Practices**
   - Develop and implement standardized clinical protocols, order sets, and decision support tools to promote guideline-adherent practices.
   - Integrate guideline-based algorithms into electronic medical record (EMR) systems to facilitate decision-making and ensure appropriate medication prescribing.
   - Establish clear referral pathways for patients who require specialty asthma care.

3. **Promote Patient Education and Engagement**
   - Provide patients with educational resources, such as asthma action plans, that align with guideline recommendations.
   - Empower patients to actively participate in their asthma management by emphasizing the importance of adherence, trigger avoidance, and self-monitoring.

4. **Utilize Quality Improvement Strategies**
   - Implement regular audits and feedback mechanisms to assess adherence to guideline-based care.
   - Identify gaps in care and implement targeted quality improvement initiatives to address them.

- Benchmark performance against national or regional quality measures for asthma care.

5. **Address Social Determinants of Health and Health Equity**
   - Recognize and address the impact of social, economic, and environmental factors on asthma outcomes.
   - Implement strategies to improve access to guideline-based care for underserved populations.
   - Collaborate with community organizations to address barriers to asthma management.

Effective implementation of guideline-based asthma care requires a multifaceted approach that engages healthcare providers, patients, and the broader healthcare system. A sustained commitment to quality improvement and a focus on addressing health disparities is essential for optimizing asthma outcomes.

LESSON TWO: MEASURING AND IMPROVING ASTHMA OUTCOMES

Measuring and improving asthma outcomes are crucial for providing high-quality, patient-centered care.

1. **Assess Asthma Control**
   - Make use of reliable resources, like the Asthma Control Test (ACT) or the Asthma Control Questionnaire (ACQ), to regularly evaluate the level of asthma control.
   - Monitor objective measures of lung function, such as peak expiratory flow (PEF) or spirometry, to track changes in airway obstruction.
   - Determine how often and how severe your asthma symptoms are, including daytime and nighttime symptoms and the use of rescue medications.

2. **Evaluate Quality of Life**
   - Utilize patient-reported outcome measures, such as the Asthma Quality of Life Questionnaire (AQLQ), to assess the

impact of asthma on a patient's physical, emotional, and social well-being.

- To meet each patient's unique needs and concerns, include patient-centered goals and priorities in the treatment plan.

3. Monitor Exacerbations and Healthcare Utilization

- Track the frequency and severity of asthma exacerbations, including the need for urgent care visits, hospitalizations, and systemic corticosteroid use.
- Evaluate the rates of emergency department visits and hospital admissions to assess the overall burden of asthma.

4. Assess Medication Adherence and Technique

- Regularly evaluate patient adherence to prescribed asthma medications, including both controller and rescue medications.
- Assess the proper use of inhalation devices, such as metered-dose inhalers (MDIs) or dry powder inhalers (DPIs), and provide education and training as needed.

5. Implement Quality Improvement Initiatives

- Establish performance measures and quality indicators aligned with evidence-based guidelines, such as the rate of guideline-recommended controller medication use or the proportion of patients with written asthma action plans.
- Determine and fix care gaps via data-driven quality improvement techniques, such as Plan-Do-Study-Act (PDSA) cycles.
- Engage healthcare teams and patients in the continuous improvement process to enhance asthma outcomes.

DISCUSSION QUESTIONS

- What strategies can you use as a healthcare provider to ensure that patients are informed about and adhere to the latest asthma management guidelines?
- How can healthcare teams effectively measure and address gaps in asthma care to improve patient outcomes?

CONCLUSION

Asthma is a long-term respiratory condition that requires careful, consistent management to enhance patient outcomes and quality of life. The goal of this course, "Asthma Education for Healthcare Providers," is to give healthcare providers the fundamental information and

 practical skills necessary for effective asthma care.

Over the six modules, healthcare providers have gained a deep understanding of asthma's pathophysiology, diagnosis, pharmacological and non-pharmacological management, patient education, emergency care, and follow-up strategies. Each module has been carefully crafted to build a robust foundation and develop advanced competencies in asthma management through a combination of theoretical learning, practical activities, and scenarios.

This course empowers healthcare providers to take a holistic and patient-centered approach to asthma management. By keeping up with the most recent regulations and consistently honing their craft, participants can significantly impact the lives of asthma patients, reducing morbidity, enhancing living standards and, in the end, saving lives. As healthcare providers, your dedication to learning and improving asthma care is commendable and vital for the health and well-being of your patients.

REFERENCES

Asthma and Allergy Foundation of America. *"Asthma Management and Education Resources."* 2023.

Boulet, L.P., and FitzGerald, J.M. *"Asthma Management and Treatment Guidelines."* UpToDate. 2023

Cloutier MM, Baptist AP, Blake KV, et al. 2020 *Focused Updates to the Asthma Management Guidelines.*

Cloutier MM, Salo PM, Akinbami LJ, Zeldin DC. *Vital Signs: Asthma in Children* - United States, 2001-2016

Global Initiative for Asthma. *"GINA Main Report 2023: Global Strategy for Asthma Management and Prevention."* 2023.

Reddel HK, Levy ML. *The GINA asthma strategy report: what's new for primary care? NPJ Prim Care Respir Med.* 2015

Szefler SJ, Zeiger RS, Haselkorn T, et al. *Economic burden of impairment in children with severe or difficult-to-treat asthma*

Schatz M, Sorkness CA, Li JT, et al. *Asthma Control Test: reliability, validity, and responsiveness in patients not previously followed by asthma specialists.* J Allergy Clin Immunol. 2006